# AMERICAN STEAM

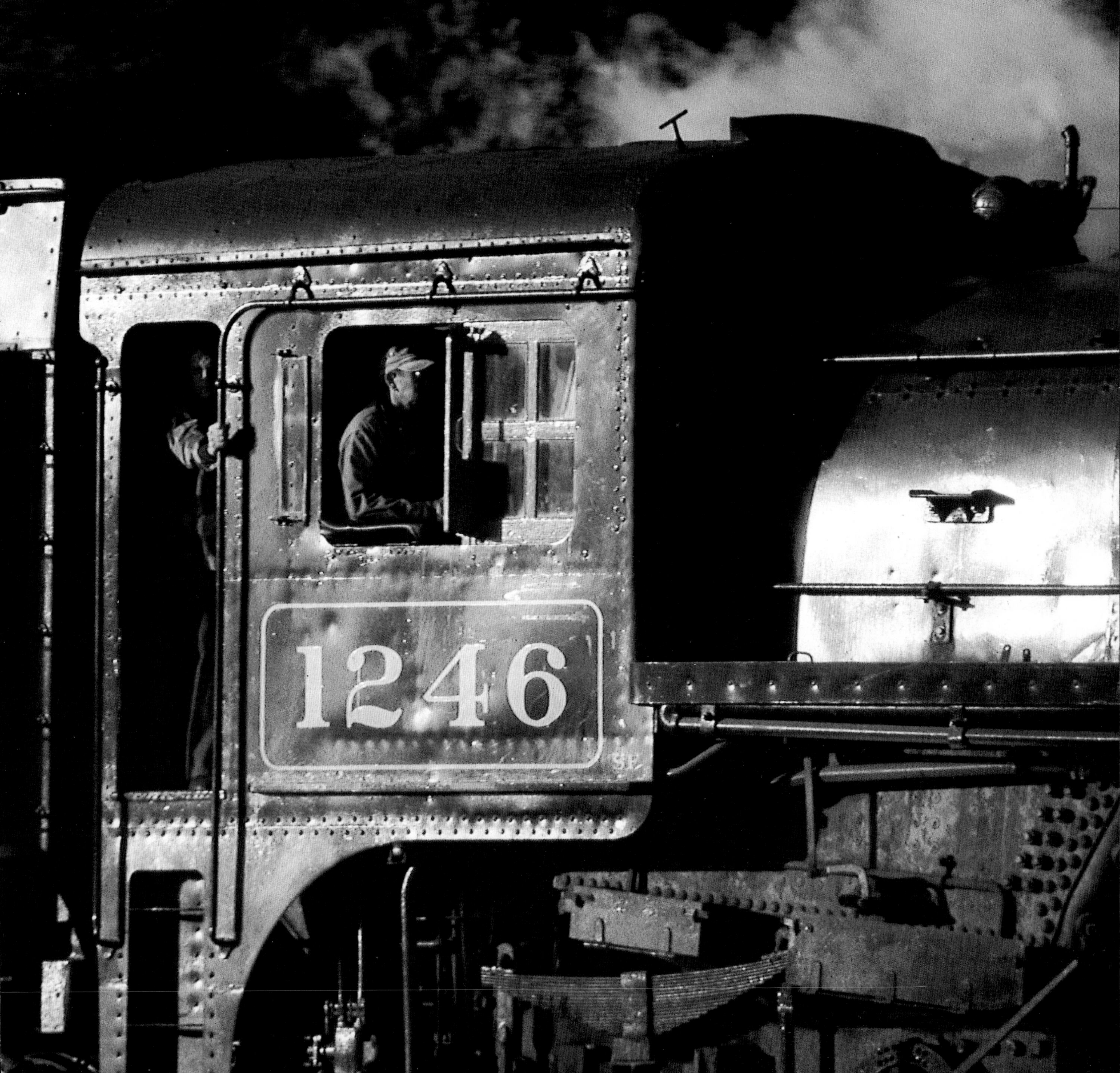
1246

# AMERICAN STEAM

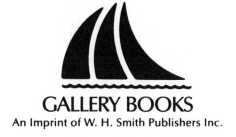

## GALLERY BOOKS

An Imprint of W. H. Smith Publishers Inc.

112·Madison Avenue New York NY 10016

## THE IMAGE BANK

111 Fifth Avenue New York NY 10003

First published in 1988 in New York by Gallery
Books, an imprint of W.H. Smith Publishers Inc.,
112 Madison Avenue, New York, N.Y. 10016

ISBN 0-8317-8803-8

For rights information about the photographs in
this book please contact:

The Image Bank
111 Fifth Avenue, New York, N.Y. 10003

Manufactured in Singapore

Produced by Robert M. Tod
Art Direction and Design by Mark Weinberg
Assistant Art Direction by Dana Shimizu Lee
Written by John M Wickre
Edited by Sheila Buff
Photo Research: Tamara Kahn
Editorial Assistance: Elizabeth Loonan

Railroads are positively the greatest blessing
that the ages have wrought for us.
They give us wings; they annihilate the toil and dust
of pilgrimage; they spiritualize travel!

**—Nathaniel Hawthorne**

Of the 160,000 steam locomotives built in America between 1830 and 1950, today only a few hundred remain in operating condition. This is the story of the development and evolution of a power system that dominated land transport for more than a century—yet disappeared in little over a decade.

The application of steam engines to rail vehicles began in Great Britain. In 1829 George Stephenson's *Rocket* established the basic form that almost all locomotives would follow until the end of the steam era. This design included a multitubular boiler, the use of exhaust steam to produce a forced draft through the firebox, and a direct connection between the piston rod and the driving wheel. Succeeding designers increased the size of the locomotive and added refinements but did not alter the basic concept.

For those unfamiliar with steam technology, it should perhaps be pointed out that what is popularly called a "steam engine" actually consists of two principal parts. The first part is a boiler to convert heat to steam by vaporizing water. The second part is the "engine" itself—the device that converts steam under pressure into mechanical energy that can be used to pump water or move a train of cars.

The romantic "chuff-chuff" of the steam locomotive is the sound of smoke and steam blasting out of the smoke stack. It is perhaps less romantic to think of this as the sound of 95 percent of the potential heat being discarded, but that thought more accurately portrays the steam locomotive's low energy efficiency.

Steam engine designers use a number of methods to retain more of the heat within the system, but not all of them can be applied to a locomotive pounding along the countryside at high speed on two slim rails. Steam does work by expanding from a high pressure and small volume into a lower pressure and larger volume. One method of increasing efficiency is by "compounding"— expanding the steam more than once before it is discarded. In a reciprocating steam engine this is done by taking the steam leaving the first, smaller-diameter cylinder, and expanding it again in a second, larger cylinder at lower pressure before it is finally exhausted.

Waste heat can be used in two other ways to increase efficiency—by heating the boiler feedwater and by superheating the steam. Heating the feedwater (the water entering the boiler) means the boiler can bring the water to the boiling point with less fuel. Further increases in efficiency can be achieved by superheating the steam between the time it leaves the boiler and the time it is used in the cylinders.

In a standard mainline engine power from the pistons is transmitted directly through the main rods to the driving wheels, which are connected together with side rods. These mainline locomotives "gear down" by using smaller drive wheels. Slow freight locomotives pulling heavy loads have smaller driving wheels than the faster passenger locomotives hauling relatively light loads. Maximum safe speed of this type of direct-drive locomotive can be calculated roughly by figuring that the highest speed in miles per hour is approximately equal to the diameter of the driving wheels in inches.

Steel drive wheels on steel rails have both advantages

and disadvantages. The principal advantage is low rolling resistance, which allows a locomotive of only a few hundred horsepower to pull a train of cars weighing hundreds of tons. A railroad car running free on a level track will roll three or four times as far as a rubber-tired motortruck of comparable weight, rolling free on a level highway. The principal mechanical disadvantage is low traction, which means that acceleration is slow, grades must not much exceed two percent (two feet in one hundred), and stopping distances are long.

Geared locomotives provide a different method of transmitting power from the pistons to the engine's drive wheels. Shay, Heisler, and Climax designs are the most common types of geared engines. All three transmit power to their drive wheels through bevel gears. They are most easily distinguished by their cylinder placement.

The Shay design uses a single set of vertical cylinders attached to one side of the boiler. The cylinders drive a crankshaft located along the side of the engine. The driveshaft in turn powers bevel gears located on the outside of the driving trucks, providing good accessibility for maintenance. Manufacturers such as the Lima Locomotive Works in Lima, Ohio, built Shays with two, three, or even four driving trucks.

The Heisler might be thought of as a V-2 design, just as gasoline engine might be a V-6 or V-8. A head-on view of a Heisler reveals mid-mounted cylinders set high on the sides of the locomotive and arranged in a 90-degree "vee" with connecting rods extending downward and inward to a driveshaft mounted centrally underneath the boiler. The driveshaft turns bevel gears on two or three

four-wheel driving trucks.

The Climax Locomotive and Machine Works manufactured a third type of geared engine. The Climax design looks much like a normal mainline engine but has its cylinders set higher than a standard engine. The cylinders are angled downward at about 40 degrees, connecting via short main rods to a cross-mounted crankshaft that turns bevel gears on the central driveshaft.

Geared engines were powerful for their size, flexible for operation on uneven track and tight curves, and able to operate on grades up to 10 percent. They were thus very successful in logging, mining, and other industrial operations, but their slow speeds and high maintenance costs precluded their use on main lines. Although American manufacturers built only 3,200 geared locomotives, many are still in existence on the rosters of museums and excursion lines.

When grades exceed 10 percent, steel wheels on steel rails do not provide sufficient adhesion for either climbing or braking, and even geared engines cannot move a train safely. The solution to this problem is the use of a third traction rail mounted in the midline of the track. The two outside rails thus serve only to carry the load, and not to provide traction. The central rack or "cog" rail is in continuous contact with spur gears mounted on the locomotive's drive axles.

New Hampshire's Mount Washington Cog Railway, completed in 1869, is said to have been the first mountain-climbing rack railroad in the world. It is still in use for excursion traffic, and it still uses steam power. Grades average 25 percent, with some stretches as steep as 37 percent.

The cog railway is not a common type. The Manitou & Pikes Peak Railway in Colorado is the only other such line in North America, and it no longer uses steam locomotives.

July 4, 1828, saw the first shovel of earth turned to begin a new canal, the Chesapeake and Ohio, and the first stone laid to begin the Baltimore and Ohio Rail Road. The canal soon lost out to the railroad as the prime transport system of a steam-powered world. The railroad provided fast, dependable, precisely scheduled transport in all seasons, oblivious to the mud that could bog down horse-drawn stagecoaches and the low water or winter ice that could end the canal and steamboat season altogether.

In the 1830s the economy of North America was primarily rural and agricultural. Most industry was small in scale, managed by its owners, and powered by water. Coal had not yet become a cheap and abundant fuel, and the steam engine was still in its infancy as a power source in America. Even in 1830, however, some American machine shops made stationary and marine steam engines. The railroad locomotive, being basically a steam engine on wheels, was a relatively simple construction project for any machine shop equipped with a large lathe and a drill press. By the mid-1830s, state legislatures had granted some 200 railroad charters with lines projected into all parts of the country. Any forward-looking machine shop owner could anticipate that steam locomotives would be a profitable addition to his current line of products.

One of the largest of these early machine shops was the West Point Foundry, located in New York City. In 1830 West Point completed the first American-built locomotive, *The Best Friend of Charleston*, at a cost of $4,000. By 1840 a dozen machine shops were producing locomotives for export as well as for domestic use. Because of this capacity for domestic manufacturing, only 120 English locomotives were ever imported in the United States, all of them between 1829 and 1841. Once American builders were able to satisfy the demand of the nation's railroads, no foreign engines were imported.

European railroads often fabricated locomotives in their own shops. This was especially true in Great Britain. In North America, however, private contractors such as West Point, M.W. Baldwin, and William Norris provided most of the locomotives. Most American railroad shops were content to remain essentially repair facilities. One of the exceptions was the Baltimore and Ohio's Mount Clare shops, which began producing locomotives in the early 1830s.

Most early American railroads served eastern coastal cities; few were more than 50 miles long. There were hundreds of railroad charters, however, and the nation's rail mileage grew from a total of 23 miles in 1830 to 2,800 miles in 1840, nearly equaling its 3,300 miles of canals. All of Europe had constructed only 1,800 miles of rail line by 1840.

The most popular engine during the period from 1835 to the early 1840s was the 4-2-0 or "six-wheel" engine. With only two driving wheels the 4-2-0 was a decidedly "slippery" engine. It was the first distinctively American type of locomotive, but its lack of traction soon ended its career in the face of competition from the engine that would become known as the "American," the 4-4-0.

Henry R. Campbell patented the 4-4-0 arrangement in 1836, and the Brooks works in Philadelphia completed the first engine in 1837. The 4-4-0 was to become the most popular wheel arrangement in the nineteenth century. Its flexible three-point suspension enabled it to operate on uneven tracks. Its four drive wheels gave it greater tractive force than the 4-2-0. It was low in first cost, durable, easy to repair, and equally suited to passenger, freight, and switching service.

The nation's first railroad boom occured in the late 1840s and early 1850s as lines extended away from the eastern seaboard to the west and south. During the 1850s total U.S. rail mileage increased by 21,000 miles, from 9,000 to 30,000. By the middle of the decade the nation had nearly as much rail mileage as the entire rest of the world, although it had no more than five percent of the total world population. By 1860 railroads served all of the states east of the Mississippi, the river itself was spanned by a railroad bridge (built by the Rock Island in 1856), and Chicago had become the nation's rail center.

Several manufacturers began to produce 4-6-0 "Ten-Wheelers" in the late 1840s, but these engines did not come into common use until the 1860s and did not rival the 4-4-0s until 1870. The 4-6-0 also had suspension problems and did not stay on rough track as well as the 4-4-0.

The discovery of gold in California and the old lure of the trans-Pacific trade led in the 1850s to the promotion of new railroads with transcontinental ambitions. The federal government surveyed a number of Pacific routes and encouraged railroad construction with land grants. The extension of railroads to the west and their projection to the Pacific changed the orientation of U.S. rail lines from north-south, following the Ohio and Mississippi rivers, to east-west, following the rail lines.

During the 1850s the 4-4-0 locomotive remained the standard, but in a new "modern" version that was more than an enlargement of the original design. This new design, generally credited to Thomas Rogers of the Rogers Works, included spread leading trucks, Stephenson link motion, and the wagon-top style of boiler. The "Rogers pattern" 4-4-0 remained the basic 4-4-0 design for the next thirty years.

By 1860 the total rail mileage of the United States had reached 31,000, but it was not yet a complete rail system. One of the biggest problems was the lack of standardization of rail gauge. "Standard gauge" was four feet, eight-and-a-half inches, but most Southern roads used five-foot gauge. A trip from Charleston to Philadelphia might require as many as eight changes of cars because of the variation in gauges from one railroad to another. Lack of bridges and transfer facilities caused further problems.

Two new wheel arrangments were introduced in the 1860s, the 2-6-0 "Mogul" and the 2-8-0 "Consolidation." Early Moguls had suspension problems much as the 4-6-0 Ten-Wheelers did, but in 1864 the superintendent of the Rogers Locomotive Works, William S. Hudson, patented a method of equalizing the truck and driving axles so they rode more smoothly over uneven tracks. Moguls were never widely popular, although they continued to be built into the 1920s.

Alexander Mitchell designed the first 2-8-0 in 1866 to haul anthracite coal over the steep grades of the Lehigh and Mahonoy Railroad. During the construction of the engine the Lehigh and Mahonoy merged with Lehigh Valley Railroad; the new engine was named in honor of the consolidated company. The "Consolidation" was designed for slow pusher service and only a few were built during the first decade of the design's existence. By 1875, however, many railroads saw its merits as a road engine and it soon became the most popular freight locomotive in America. Some 33,000 were constructed between its introduction in 1866 and 1950.

Despite the introduction of new wheel arrangement, wood-burning 4-4-0 locomotives continued to be the most popular engines during the 1860s. Most railroads preferred to run relatively light trains at slow speeds. From the 1850s into the 1890s passenger trains averaged about 25 miles an hour and freight trains 10 miles an hour. The "American" still served well in such light use.

By 1865 wood was going out of style as a fuel, however, as eastern forests were logged off and trains began to move westward onto the treeless prairies. By 1870 the percentage of locomotives burning wood had dropped to 50 percent, and by 1880 wood was no longer in common use on most mainline roads. On logging and secondary lines where wood was plentiful, however, it remained a viable fuel as long as steam was viable. The last common carrier to burn wood was probably the Mississippi and Alabama Railroad, which continued to use wood as late as 1949.

The first major rail construction after the Civil War was the transcontinental line of the combined Union Pacific (building west from Omaha, Nebraska) and Central Pacific (building east from Sacramento, California). The CP/UP transcontinental set new standards for flimsy construction, watered stock, and "hell on wheels" construction camps. A widely publicized "gold-spike" ceremony joined the two lines at Promontory Point, Utah, on May 10, 1869.

In the half-century after the Civil War a dozen states joined the Union, from Nebraska in 1867 to Arizona in 1912. The CP/UP line was only the first of dozens of railroads that moved ahead of the line settlement. Rail mileage in the Great Plains and Mountain West (west of the line from North Dakota through Texas) increased from less than 1,000 miles in 1865 to 90,000 miles in 1915. As many as 50 million buffaloes still roamed the plains at the beginning of this period. Ahead of the rails, horses and men provided power. Teams of horse-drawn scoops graded the line, and horse-drawn wagons carried supplies and materials to the contractors and surveyors.

Between 1870 and 1872 U.S. railroads constructed 19,000 miles of track; total U.S. mileage increased from 53,000 miles in 1870 to 93,000 miles in 1880. The total number of men employed by the nation's railroads increased from 163,000 in 1870 to 419,000 in 1880.

It was the 1880s, however, that saw the peak of railroad construction in the United States, with a total of 71,000 miles of track laid in the decade, including nearly 12,000 miles in 1882 and an all-time high of almost 13,000 miles in 1887. Most of this construction was in the west and southwest. The Northern Pacific and Canadian Pacific completed transcontinental lines in 1883 and 1885, respectively.

Perhaps the most important advance during the 1880s came in the form of standardization, expecially the changeover to standard gauge and standard time. In 1880 20 percent of the nation's rail mileage was in other than the standard 4 foot, 8½ inch standard gauge. At the beginning of the decade most of this diversity occurred in such western narrow-gauge lines as the Denver and Rio Grande and in the 12,000 miles of five-foot gauge found in the Old South. Without a standard gauge cars could not be interchanged between railroads. Freight had to be unloaded and reloaded at each change of gauge, wasting time and money and making it impossible to have a truly integrated national rail network.

A number of important roads changed to standard gauge by the mid-1880s. The changeover was never simple because it could not be done gradually but had to be carried out over hundreds of miles of line at one time. Shop crews had to modify locomotives and cars at the same time that track gangs moved the rails. One of the most publicized changeovers occurred in 1886, when southern lines changed more than 13,000 miles of track to standard gauge over a two-day period.

The changeover to standard time was somewhat simpler, but no less important. Running a nation-wide system was no easy task when every station could set its own local sun time. Times could vary even within a single city—Pittsburgh, for example, having six different times. The change to standard time went into effect at noon on Sunday, November 18, 1883.

The steam locomotives themselves remained basically unchanged during this decade, as 4-4-0 "American" engines continued to supply most of the country's motive power, with various sizes of the 2-6-0 "Mogul" and 2-8-0 "Consolidation" filling out most rosters. Whatever the wheel arrangement chosen, each railroad deveeloped standard classes of locomotives suited to its own unique needs. This practice helped lower repair and inventory expenses.

Thus locomotive designs in the 1880s became standardized within individual railroads, but no standard designs were acceptable to all railroads. It is ironic that the railroad industry, which had so much to do with the developmentof modern high-speed mass production, never developed mass production for its own motive power. Each railroad believed that it had unique needs that could not be met by standard designs. Manufacturers built locomotives on demand, on a custom basis. Small orders were common, often no more than ten or twenty engines at a time. The purchasing railroad provided the specifications and also provided its own inspectors to insure that the designs were followed.

The decade of the 1890s saw the beginnings of major changes in both railroad organization and locomotive design. With the completion to the Pacific of James J. Hill's Great Northern line in 1893, the basic outlines of the nation's rail net were essentially complete. The railroad industry changed from a pattern of expansion and competition to one of consolidation and systems-building. The financial panic of 1893 slowed construction and caused the bankruptcy of a number of lines. Less than 30,000 miles of track were laid in this decade, as the total rail mileage in the United States grew from 164,000 miles in 1890 to 193,000 miles in 1900.

The most spectacular growth after 1890 came in the locomotives themselves. In 1890 the 4-4-0 and 4-6-0 engines used in passenger service weighed perhaps 50 tons with tenders. A typical 2-8-0 freight engine might weigh 75 tons. By 1900 a typical road engine weighed 60 to 100 tons. This trend was to continue until clearance restrictions and the limitations of track capacity ended the race with locomotives over 100 feet long, weighing as much as 400 tons.

One of the reasons for this increase was the need for longer and faster trains. Labor, fuel, and capital costs could all be reduced when one heavy engine could do the work of three small engines. At first these large engines showed little gain in power-per-pound over the machines built in the 1850s. Designers raised steam pressures to 200 pounds per inch, but this called for thicker boiler plate. Engines remained relatively ponderous.

Maunufacturers not only increased the size of the common types of engines already in use, but they designed several new wheel arrangements, basically by adding a two-wheel trailing truck to the styles already in use. Before 1900 the 4-4-0 "American," 4-6-0 "Ten-Wheeler," and 2-6-0 "Mogul" designs were most common in passenger service, while the heavy 2-8-0 "Consolidation" and 2-10-0 "Decapod" styles provided

most of the freight engines. The addition of the two-wheel trailing truck to these designs between 1895 and 1903 produced the 4-4-2 "Atlantic," the 4-6-2 "Pacific," and 2-6-2 "Prairie" passenger engines and the 2-8-2 "Mikado" and 2-10-2 "Santa Fe" freight engines.

In these new engines the designers placed the firebox over the trailing truck above the frame. The firebox thus could be made as wide as allowed by side clearance restrictions. The increase in firebox size and grate area permitted larger boilers and overall greater power per machine (though not any greater thermal efficiency). Total weights increased to 100 tons or more, with boiler diameters up to 80 inches.

By 1890 the men who designed the engines had changed along with their engines, as university-trained engineers replaced the old-line master mechanics and locomotive builders and analytical, scientific methods replaced the old rule-of-thumb methods of designing locomotives.

Locomotive factories changed at the same time. Just as the ordinary machine shop had been replaced by the locomotive factory specializing in railroad engines, so too was the old factory replaced by new facilities with electric cranes and overhead clearances high enough to lift an entire finished locomotive over nearby engines still in the process of assembly. New large factories required massive capital investment. Baldwin, Pittsburgh, Cooke, and a few other builders opened new factories about this time. The smaller builders that could not afford such facilities simply went out of business.

Railroad structures had to change along with the

engines. The higher weights and lengths required that roundhouses and turntables be extended or replaced, and heavier rail laid to carry the increased tonnage.

One new type of engine began to be produced in this decade: the articulated style with a hinged frame and two sets of driving wheels. The hinged frame permitted large boilers while retaining the ability to negotiate tight curves. Beginning with Alco's 0-6-6-0 exhibited at the 1904 St. Louis Exposition, articulateds were built with a variety of wheel arrangements. The most popular in the early years of the century were the 2-6-6-2, first built by Baldwin for the Great Northern in 1906, and the 2-8-8-2, first built by Baldwin for the Southern Pacific in 1909.

These early articulated were normally compounds, with the steam being used first in the rear high-pressure cylinders and expanded again in the front low-pressure cylinders. By using steam twice a compound engine improved fuel economy at the expense of higher first cost and increased maintenance.

The major reason for the demise of the compound engine was the emergenceof the superheater, which increased power by 25 percent, but added little to the cost or weight of the locomotive. Superheaters raised steam temperature and energy without increasing pressure by using a group of small-diameter tubes to carry steam back through the fire tubes of the boiler for reheating. The concept had been known since the early years of the steam engine, but had been little used on locomotives due to problems of packing and lubrication. By 1902 Wilhelm Schmidt, a German engineer, had solved most of these problems. After 1910 all new road engines were equipped with superheaters, and many older ones were rebuilt to use them. There was no longer any need to put up with the increased complexity of compound cylinders, and the concept was little used after this time.

Other technical improvements in the first years of the century included all-steel, radial-stay boilers, piston valves, and outside valve gears. All of these ideas had been used earlier but had not been accepted as standard practice. The Walschaerts outside valve gear had been invented in 1844. It came into common use after 1905 not because it was superior in steam distribution (which it was) but rather because the increasingly heavy engines of the time allowed little room for the older Stephenson valve gear.

As the new larger engines became popular many of the older wheel arrangements lost favor or were dropped entirely. The 4-4-0 was the first to be dropped. Manufacturers had built more than 25,000 "Americans" beginning in the 1840s, but constructed none after about 1905.

In 1916 the U.S. rail network reached its all-time high of 254,000 miles—seven times the mileage in existence at the end of the Civil War. During these years the nation's economy had evolved from a rural agricultural focus to an industrial competitor of international importance. Its population had nearly tripled, increasing from 36 million to 103 million. Railroads directly employed nearly two million workers, one out of twenty-five of those in the work force, or an average of more than six workers per mile of line. Many more worked in related industries.

These were good years for steam locomotive builders,

but several competitors now appeared to challenge the supremacy of both steam as a power source and steel rails as a method of transport. For a time it seemed that the electric locomotive would prove to be a viable replacement for steam. A number of eastern roads electrified their operations in densely populated urban areas or through tunnels. The Great Northern electrified its Cascade tunnel line in 1909. In 1915 the Milwaukee Road electrified several hundred miles of its western trackage through the mountains of Montana, Idaho and Washington.

The rail motor car became a significant competitor of the steam locomotive at this time because it allowed companies to end the use of steam for passenger runs on little-used branch lines. Another user of internal combustion engines was soon to have a much greater impact on railroad usage: the use of the private automobile began to cut passenger revenues at the same time that railroad taxes were beginning to be used to build public roads.

Total U.S. railroad mileage slowly declined after 1916 as track began to be abandoned faster than it was laid. From the high of 254,000 miles in 1916, trackage fell to 253,000 miles in 1920 and 249,000 miles in 1930. Railroad employment rose to 2,000,000 by 1920. More ominously, average railroad wages in 1920 were 33 percent higher than those in manufacturing. Another ominous statistic was the number of motor vehicle registrations, which increased from 3.4 million in 1916 to 23 million in 1929.

It is perhaps not surprising, then, that railroad management in the 1920s showed an increased interest in large engines that could increase train tonnage and reduce labor costs. Competition from motor trucks and buses also became a factor in this decade, and railroads tried to meet this competition by speeding up both freight and passenger service.

Perhaps the most important contribution to locomotive design at this time came from the "Super Power" concept pioneered by Lima's chief engineer, W.E. Woodard. In 1925 Lima built the world's first 2-8-4, a "demonstrator" Super Power engine formed by adding a four-wheel trailing truck to the 2-8-2 wheel arrangement to support a large firebox and grate area.

The high-horsepower engine with large firebox and four-wheel trailing truck soon set a new standard in locomotive design. Several new wheel arrangements using these features soon appeared, including the 2-10-4 "Texas" freight locomotive in 1925 and the 4-6-4 "Hudson" passenger engine in 1927.

The Northern Pacific pioneered two wheel arrangements during this period, the 4-8-4 "Northern" in 1926 and the 2-8-8-4 "Yellowstone" in 1929. The "Northern" was a dual purpose engine that rode well and was powerful enough for both fast freight and heavy passenger service. One of the NP's Northerns was the famous Timken 1111 or *Four Aces*, built in 1930 by Alco for Timken as a demonstration engine to prove the potential of Timken's roller bearings for use on locomotive driving axles. The roller bearings were so low in friction that three women secretaries were able to pull the 355-ton engine back and forth on a level track.

Other technological changes in this decade included

the use of oil fuel to replace coal on western lines, the introduction of one-piece cast-steel frames, the reintroduction of the feedwater heater, and the use of grease guns to replace the engineer's long-spouted oil can.

The depression of the 1930s caused a drastic decline in freight tonnage and passenger revenues, but the effect on the steam locomotive industry can perhaps best be illustrated by a single set of statistics: after years of building 1,000 to 2,000 locomotives annually, in 1932 the entire industry received orders for five engines. Although production increased to three or four hundred a year as the depression lifted, the industry never really recovered.

The depression did not dampen completely the industry's interest in new designs, however. In 1936, for example, both the Union Pacific and the Norfolk & Western designed high-speed articulated engines. The UP's 4-6-6-4 "Challenger" class locomotives proved equally adaptable to both passenger and fast freight service. They could haul 3,700-ton trains at speeds up to 70 miles per hour.

The biggest obstacle to further innovation, however, was the simple fact that by the mid-1930s designers had made the conventional reciprocating locomotive just about as powerful and efficient as it was possible to make it. The basic concept had not changed in a century. The horizontal, multitubular, fire-tube boiler and the direct connection between the piston rod and the driving wheels were distinguishing features of mainline steam locomotives from 1830 until the end of steam. What had changed most was size, from the 4.5-ton *Best Friend of*

*Charleston* in 1830 to the 400- to 600-ton monsters of the 1930s and 1940s. A single locomotive could now produce as much as 7,000 horsepower and pull 150-car freight trains weighing as much as 12,000 tons.

The locomotive boiler was the principal hindrance to further development. Boiler pressures had increased to more than 300 pounds per square inch, but further increases in pressure were not possible without new boiler and firebox designs. There were some alternatives but all posed insurmountable cost, weight, or maintenance problems.

As the United States emerged from the depression of the 1930s the railroad industry faced the demands of a new war with total rail mileage that had decreased slightly from the first war's 254,000 miles to the 1940's 234,000. Total numbers of locomotives had decreased as well, as smaller numbers of more powerful locomotives replaced the lighter engines of an earlier era. Overall, the nation's railroads had 33 percent fewer employees, 25 percent fewer freight cars and 30 percent fewer passenger cars and locomotives. The Northern Pacific's roster, for example, contained more than 1,400 engines in 1920, but listed only 841 in 1940.

The roadbed that supported the new heavy power now included nearly 94,000 miles of rails that weighed more than 100 pounds to the yard. Centralized train control and other advances in signaling helped the new power and heavier track carry more trains on fewer miles of rail with fewer employees.

The nation's railroads prospered during the war years, despite wage increases. Perhaps the most impressive locomotives built during the war years were the Union Pacific "Big Boys" constructed by Alco in 1941 and 1944. These giants weighed 604 tons, measured over 132 feet long, and put out 7,000 horsepower under full steam. In 1945 Alco built for the New York Central a series of 4-8-4s that averaged 22,000 miles per month, and included one engine that set a world's record by averaging 28,000 miles per month. Despite this record the New York Central dieselized rapidly after 1948, the year it bought its last steamer.

The end came quickly after the war. Lines such as the Southern Railway had bought few steam locomotives after 1930, making the decision to dieselize an easy one. Companies with modern steam power or with their own sources of coal were the last to capitulate. By the late 1950s few steam locomotives remained on Class I railroads, and most of those were stored on scrap lines, or set aside for emergency use. By the early 1960s almost all were scrapped, including some with as much as a million miles of useful life still in them. Some were used for such ignominious purposes as providing steam for thawing ore cars or for keeping passenger cars warm while they were waiting to be pulled by the new diesels.

The elimination of steam also eliminated steam-related structures and jobs. Water tanks, boiler-washing plants, and coaling stations disappeared. Boilermakers and steamfitters were no longer needed. More efficient engines, new ways of handling freight, mechanized track maintenance equipment, and computerized signaling and train control also tended to eliminate jobs. Despite an overall increase in the nation's population, railroad employment declined from over 2,000,000 in 1920 to less than 900,000 in 1960 to approximately 346,000 in 1985.

In the 120 years from 1830 to the early 1950s the American locomotive industry had produced perhaps 160,000 steam engines. The engines became larger and more powerful over the years, but the same basic concept served for the entire steam era. The sound and smell of steam and the sight of flashing rods had become a part of millions of lives. It should not be surprising, therefore, that a population who grew up with steam did not put it aside as lightly as the railroad companies.

The interest in steam railroading is not just an interest in huge full-size mainline engines but exists in a spectrum of guises, from N-scale model railroads operating at a scale of 1:160, through the common HO train sets, live steam models in a variety of scales up to 1½-inch scale (one-eighth full scale), narrow-gauge industrial and excursion lines in gauges from 18 inches to three feet, to full-size standard-gauge lines using engines varying in size from tiny industrial tank locomotives to working "Big Boy" articulateds.

Not all the steam locomotives ended up on scrap lines, of course. Railroad public-relations departments got a great deal of publicity out of the donation of engines to cities for static display in parks. These tended quickly to lose their cab glass, builder's plates, bells, and any other parts that could be smashed or pried loose. Parts exposed to water rusted, froze, and cracked.

Other engines ended up in static displays in museums, not used but at least not exposed to vandalism and water. Museums restored a few to operating condition with various degrees of historical authenticity. Excursion lines, scenic railroads, theme parks, zoos, and other commercial ventures saved a few more engines from the scrap heap. In these lucky few, live steam again drives pistons to propel cars on steel rails, and recreates at least part of the time when steam moved the world.

*As we rush, as we rush in the train,*

*The trees and the houses go wheeling back,*

*But the starry heavens above that plain*

*Come flying on our track.*

**—James Thomson**

*Engine #201 framed by a depot, baggage cart, and milk can, reminiscent of the days when "milk run" meant a train that stopped at every small station in dairy country to pick up milk and cream.*

*Brightly painted engine #8 in front of
Old Tucson's freight office in Arizona.*

*The Reno alongside Old Tucson's depot. Note the crates, barrels, and sacks
of potatoes and pinto beans. The station agent at a real depot would probably
be in big trouble for leaving such freight exposed to weather and thieves.*

*A left-side view of the* Reno. *The 4-4-0 "American" was the most popular wheel arrangement in the nineteenth century. American manufacturers built more than 25,000 4-4-0s from the 1840s until about 1905.*

*Old Tucson's* Reno, *an ex-Virginia and Truckee 4-4-0 built in 1872 that was said to be the oldest operating steam locomotive in the United States until the Smithsonian's recent restoration of the 1831* John Bull. *The smokestack is a "bonnet" or "sunflower" type with a wire mesh covering to catch sparks and cinders.*

*One of two Baldwin engines with boiler-mounted water tanks hauling passengers along the line of the Roaring Camp and Big Trees Narrow-Gauge Railroad near Felton, California. The train climbs an 8 percent grade through a redwood forest and up a double switchback to the top of Bear Mountain.*

*Engine #4, a 2-6-6-2 tank engine, steaming upgrade at Castro Point, California.*

*An 0 – 6 – 0 switcher at Castro Point, California. American manufacturers built over 15,000  0 – 6 – 0s, mostly between 1900 and the 1940s.*

*A small industrial 2-6-2 with boiler-mounted tank, now on display at Castro Point, California.*

*An overhead view of the V-cylindered Heisler #5 at Castro Point, California.*
*This geared locomotive was probably used on a mountainous logging or mining line.*

*Engine #1744, an ex-Southern Pacific
2-6-0 built by Baldwin in 1901, on the
Heber Creeper railroad between
Heber City and Vivian Park, Utah.*

*Roaring Camp's engine #1, a two-truck
Shay geared locomotive, built by Lima in 1912
for the Coal Processing Corporation.
The narrow-gauge railroad operates near
Felton in northern California.*

*Engine #104, a narrow-gauge Baldwin 2-6-2T, filling its boiler-mounted
water tank before pulling out with Black Hills Central Railroad's "1880 Train,"
between Keystone Junction and Hill City, South Dakota.*

*Engine #40, built by Baldwin in 1881, at the Ghost Town water tank of the Roaring Camp and Big Trees Narrow Gauge Railroad
near Felton, California. In the nineteenth century such water tanks were spaced an average of ten miles apart.*

*An unidentified 2-6-2T industrial locomotive awaiting restoration somewhere in Oregon.*

*Engine #105 endures the elements and hopes for restoration on a siding in Oregon.*

*Engine #7, built by the Lima Locomotive Works, Lima, Ohio, one of the few major locomotive manufacturers located outside of the northeastern United States.*

*A V-cylindered Heisler geared locomotive, now operating on the Roaring Camp and Big Trees Narrow Gauge Railroad in California.*

*Engine #100, a 2-8-2
built by Baldwin in 1926
for the Santa Maria
Railroad, seen here
pulling an excursion
train on the Heber
Creeper railroad near
Heber City, Utah.*

41

*Engine #200, an ex-Southern Pacific 4-6-0 built by Cooke in 1896, now operated by the Texas State Railroad between Palestine and Rusk.*

*A head-on portrait of engine #40, a 2-8-2 now operating on the Valley Railroad Company's tracks in Essex, Connecticut.*

*Engine #1, a 4-4-0 built by Mason in 1876,*
*at Greenfield Village, Dearborn, Michigan.*

*Engine #40 steams through a residential area on a beautiful day.*
*The black, sooty smoke the engine makes illustrates*
*why people didn't like to live along the rail line.*

*Engine #9, an 0-6-0 switcher built by Alco in 1942, at the New Hope*
*Steam Railway and Museum at New Hope, Pennsylvania. It probably did not*
*have yellow running boards and hand rails in its working days.*

*Engine #4 at Castro Point, California. Small for an articulated, this 2-6-6-2 engine*
*with boiler-mounted water tank was once used in logging service by the Clover Valley Lumber Co.*

*A train winds through the beautiful autumn foliage of the Connecticut River Valley
on the Valley Railroad Company's tracks near Essex.*

*Steamtown's #1246 4-6-2
steams around a bend in a
Vermont autumn on the
Bellows Falls to Rutland route.
The Canadian Pacific built this
engine at its Montreal shops in
1946. The Steamtown
collection was located in
Vermont from 1966 until 1984,
when it was moved to
Scranton, Pennsylvania.*

*Engine #1009 at a crossing in Nova Scotia, Canada.*

The **Three-Spot**, *first engine on the newly formed Duluth and Iron Range Railroad in 1883.*
*The little Baldwin 2-6-0 weighed 75,000 pounds, hardly one-tenth the weight of the 2-8-8-4 articulated*
*that would be among the last steam engines used on the successor DM&IR.*

*Engine #52 of the White Pass and Yukon Route, a narrow-gauge common carrier built during the 1898-1900 Alaska Gold Rush and still in operation transporting passengers and freight between Skagway, Alaska and Whitehorse, British Columbia.*

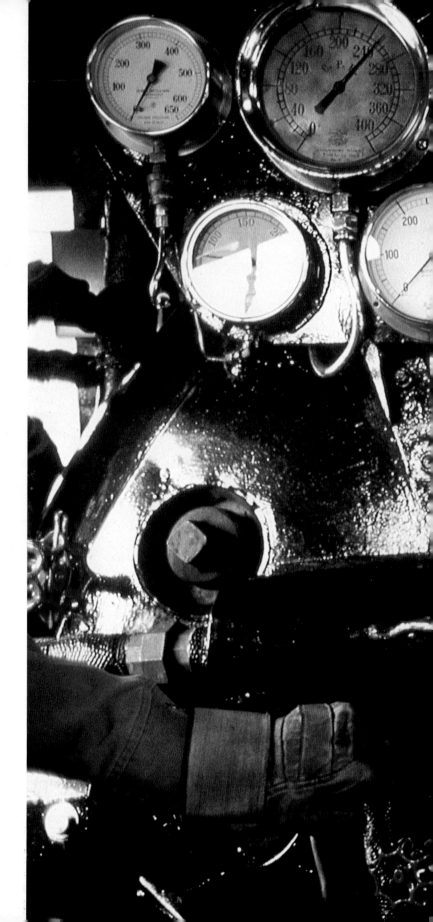

*A glimpse at the cab and gauges of a "Royal Hudson" 4-6-4 in Vancouver, British Columbia.*

A view looking forward along
a modern 4-8-4 provides a
good illustration of the
complex mechanism needed
to change the straight-line
motion of the piston in the
cylinder into the rotary motion
of the wheels.

The crosshead provides a flexible connection between the piston and the main rod that provides power to the drive wheels, while the valve gear controls admission of steam to the cylinder at the right point in the power cycle.

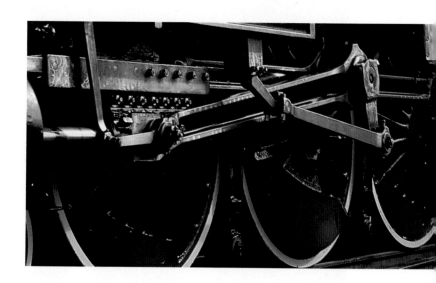

The wheels and rods of a Royal Hudson in Vancouver, British Columbia. This locomotive is a "Royal" because it is of the type that carried King George VI across Canada in 1939.

In this close-up, the crosshead and wheel of a locomotive in Tennessee can be clearly seen. The crosshead is used to convert the linear motion of the piston to the circular motion of the wheel.

*The engineer prepares to get Canadian Pacific engine #1278 under way. This 4-6-2 was built in 1947 in Montreal. It was replaced by a diesel when it still had years of useful life ahead of it.*

*Canadian Pacific engine #1278, a 4-6-2 built by the company's Montreal shops about 1947. A water capacity of 9,600 gallons was average for medium-sized engines. Early tenders carried only perhaps 2,000 to 3,000 gallons, while tenders for the largest locomotives at the end of the age of steam carried as much as 25,000 gallons.*

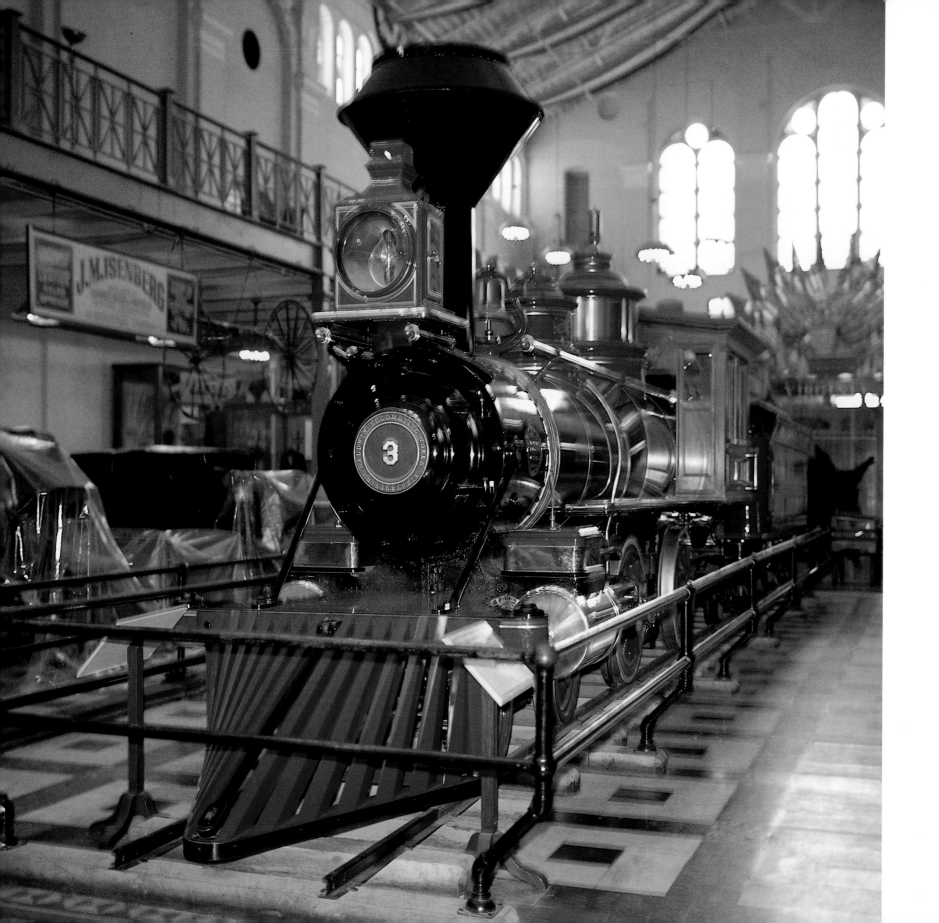

This restored dining car in Orillia, Ontario, hints at
the elegance of the bygone days of steam travel.

The St. Paul & Pacific's engine #1, the William Crooks, built by
Smith and Jackson in 1861, and now on display at the
Lake Superior Museum of Transportation in Duluth, Minnesota.

Baldwin engine #3 is beautifully preserved at the
Smithsonian Institution in Washington, D.C. The locomotive is part of
an exhibit that recreates the Centennial Exposition of
1876; it was the ultimate in transportation technology in its time.

*Ready to take on passengers at Smith's Creek station at Greenfield Village in Dearborn, Michigan. The passenger platform by the locomotive is a modern addition. Engine #3 is a Mason-Fairlie 0-6-4T tank engine built in 1873 for the Hecla and Torch Lake Railway Company, a mining railroad. It originally was built to 4-ft. 1-inch gauge, but was changed to the standard 4-ft. 8.5-inch gauge in 1907.*

*Baldwin engine #8 under restoration at the Portola Railroad Museum, Portola, California.*

*The view from the top of the B&O Museum's 1884 roundhouse, once part of the Baltimore & Ohio's shops in Mt. Clare, Maryland. The wooden cover over the turntable pit conforms to the original design. The museum's collections include an 1856 4-4-0, a Jersey Central "Camelback" with mid-mounted cab, and a streamlined C&O 4-6-4 "Hudson." The entrance to the museum is through 1830 Mt. Clare Station, the nation's first railroad station. The B&O established the museum in 1953, and it is now supported by the B&O's successor, the Chessie System (or CSX). The museum is the largest rail exhibit in the U.S.*

*A Baldwin 0-6-0 switch engine on static display at Church Street Station, Orlando, Florida.*

*A small tank-type engine taking on water from a wooden water tank at Fort Wilderness, Orlando, Florida.*

*The "Chattanooga Choo-Choo" nickname was applied informally to the Cincinnati Southern Railroad, the country's first city-owned mainline railway. Its 338 miles of track between Cincinnati, Ohio, and Chattanooga, Tennessee, began operation in 1880. It was also known as the "Rat-Hole Division" due to its 27 tunnels.*

*A far pass from Alaska: ex-White Pass & Yukon 2-8-2 #190, built by Baldwin in 1943, now operates on a three-mile loop on the "Tweetsie Railroad" as part of a theme park that features a re-created Western town, Indian raids, and train hold-ups, in the Blue Ridge Mountains of North Carolina between Boone and Blowing Rock.*

*Engine #1,* Anaka, *one of two Porter 2-4-0s built in 1943 for the Carbon Limestone Company, now operated on the island of Maui by the Lahaina, Kaanapali & Pacific Railroad, a recreation of an early Hawaiian sugar-cane railway.*

*The* Myrtle, *on the Lahaina, Kaanapali & Pacific Railroad on the island of Maui in Hawaii, pulls coaches patterned after the 1890s Kalakauan cars of the Hawaii Rail Road.*

*The* Col. Teague *was built in the Mount Washington Cog Railway's own shops in 1972. It was named for the line's founder, whose family owned the railway from 1869 to 1981.*

*On the Mount Washington Cog Railway the engines push their passenger cars up the mountain and then back down in reverse. The inclined boiler keeps the boiler water as nearly level as possible on the steep grades. All braking comes from steam compression in the engine's four cylinders.*

*A good view of the central rack rail on New Hampshire's Mount Washington Cog Railway, the world's first mountain-climbing railroad. With grades averaging 25 percent, and some as steep as 37 percent, steel wheels on steel rails do not provide sufficient traction for either climbing or braking. On a "cog" railway the rack rail is in continuous contact with spur gears mounted on the locomotive's drive axles.*

*A lonely track stretches seemingly to infinity through New Mexico.*

*Engine #476 of the Durango and Silverton narrow-gauge former mining railway on a summer trip into the Rockies.*

*An exported engine reimported: Engine #44, a 2-8-0 manufactured by Baldwin in 1921 for the International Railways of Central America, now in use on the Georgetown Loop Railroad near Georgetown, Colorado. The Georgetown Loop was part of a Colorado Central (later Colorado & Southern) line opened in 1884 and abandoned in 1939. The Colorado Historical Society reconstructed the loop and its 100-foot-high Devils Gate Bridge in the 1970s.*

*A look into the cab of engine #44. The rear-facing headlight indicates the engine was used in switching service.*

*Engine #478 at one end of its winding, mountainous path between Durango and Silverton in the Colorado Rockies.*

*A ride behind one of the Durango and Silverton's steam locomotives is a trip into the rough-and-ready days of the great silver rush of the 1870s and 1880s. This narrow-gauge line operated at elevations of over 10,000 feet; it was frequently closed by the Rocky Mountain winter weather.*

*Engine #478 on a short-radius curve on the Durango to Silverton run in Colorado.*

*A Denver & Rio Grande Western train snakes along a mountain grade. This restored mining railroad is one of the most popular in America.*

*Engine #476 works a train through the summertime mountains near Durango, Colorado.*

*Engine #478 with snow plow, ready for the long, snowy
winter on the Durango and Silverton route.*

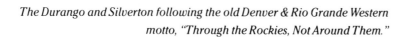

*The Durango and Silverton following the old Denver & Rio Grande Western
motto, "Through the Rockies, Not Around Them."*

*The rear headlight of VSP&SS engine #105 shines through the dusk from a side track.*

Red was once a common caboose color, and the "little red caboose" was the final car in every freight train, serving as conductor's office, observation tower, and trainmen's "home away from home" on long runs. In later years, the red tended to disappear as railroads painted their cabooses in their line's standard colors. Today the caboose itself is disappearing as railroads eliminate them wherever the law allows.

# INDEX OF PHOTOGRAPHERS